this
·little·barron's·
book belongs to

....

....

First edition for the United States and Canada published 1999
by Barron's Educational Series, Inc.

Copyright © Penny Dann 1998

First published in Great Britain by Orchard Books in 1998 under the
title *Incey Wincey Spider*.

All inquiries should be addressed to:
Barron's Educational Series, Inc.
250 Wireless Boulevard
Hauppauge, New York 11788
http://www.barronseduc.com

Library of Congress Catalog Card No.: 98-72773
International Standard Book No. 0-7641-0857-3

Printed in Italy

987654321

Eensy Weensy Spider

Penny Dann

• little • barron's •

The eensy weensy spider ...

climbed up the
water spout.

Down came
the rain ...

and washed the spider out!

Out came
the sun

and dried up
all the rain.

and the eensy weensy
spider ...

climbed up the
spout again.